D1265376

IN CONGRE

nous Declaration of the

When in the Course of human events it becomes necessary

e separate and equal station to which the Laws of Nature and of

them to the separation. ——————— We hold these

among these are Life, Liberty and the pursuit of Happiness

, — That whenever any Form of Government becomes destructi

uch principles and organizing its powers in such form, as

ished should not be changed for light and transient causes;

elves by abolishing the forms to which they are accustomed.

bsolute Despotism, it is their right, it is their duty, to throw

nies; and such is now the necessity which constrains them to

nd usurpations, all having in direct object the establishment

used his Assent to Laws, the most wholesome and necessary

SS, JULY 4, 1776.

teen united States of Am

u people to dissolve the political bands which have connected them
ture's God entitle them, a decent respect to the opinions of ma
to be self-evident, that all men are created equal, that they are
That to secure these rights, Governments are instituted among
these ends, it is the Right of the People to alter or to abolish it,
m shall seem most likely to effect their Safety and Happin
accordingly all experience hath shewn, that mankind are m
t when a long train of abuses and usurpations, pursuing inv
ch Government, and to provide new Guards for their future
their former Systems of Government. The history of the p
absolute Tyranny over these States. To prove this, let F
public good. ———— He has forbidden his Governors t

Library of Congress Catalog Card Number: 57-7537
Printed in the United States of America

16   17

SBN 531-00458-9

FRANKLIN WATTS, INC.
845 Third Avenue, New York, N.Y. 10022

THE FIRST BOOK OF
AMERICAN HISTORY

BY

HENRY STEELE COMMAGER

PICTURES BY

LEONARD EVERETT FISHER

1.

Imagine discovering a new world!

For thousands of years America was hidden from history. The rest of the world, Europe and ancient Asia, knew nothing about the continents we call North and South America, nothing about the Indians who roamed over their vast plains and river valleys, and who had built up great civilizations in Mexico and Peru. Europeans thought that there was nothing between Europe and Asia but an endless expanse of water.

Then, just about five hundred years ago, Europe discovered America.

It was far and away the greatest discovery in history. There had never been anything like it before; there will never be anything like it again.

The great discovery came in 1492 when an Italian sailor, Christopher Columbus, sailed three tiny ships under the flag of Spain all the way across the Atlantic Ocean to the Caribbean Sea. He did not expect to find a new world. When, after an eternity of sailing across the ocean, he sighted land on the morning of October 12, 1492, he thought he had reached the Indies. To this day we call the islands that he discovered the West Indies, and we still call the copper-colored natives of the New World Indians.

First a new world, then a new race of men! Surely few things in history have been as exciting as the discovery of the Indians. They had made their way to America about 25,000 years before, working their way from island to island across the frozen waters between Siberia

1

and Alaska, drifting down the west coast of America, fanning out to south and east until in the end they were all over the continent. There were never very many of them — maybe a million, or even fewer, in the whole of what is now North America. As they spread out over the continent, they divided up into hundreds of tribes that differed from each other just as countries like the United States and Mexico or France and Italy differ from each other now. Some of the Indian tribes, like the fierce Sioux of the Plains, were warlike and lived by hunting or by fighting other tribes. Others were peaceful farmers, like the Pueblos who built adobe cities in what is now New Mexico. Still others lived by farming and hunting and fishing like the Hurons of the East, who gave their name to one of America's greatest lakes.

What would America be without these Indian names — the most beautiful that any land has ever had! Susquehanna, Potomac, Mississippi — names of great rivers. Huron, Michigan, Cayuga, Seneca — names of mighty lakes. Ohio, Illinois, Dakota — names of states. Names like music, when we say them over.

And what would America have been without the Indians themselves, with their magnificent feathered headdresses, their colorful blankets, their bows and arrows and wampum belts, their wigwams and moccasins and birch-bark canoes that cut through the water like steel ploughs — their poetry and their history.

The first white men to come to America were the Spaniards. They came mostly to the islands of the Caribbean and to Mexico, and from there they spread north into the high dry lands of New Mexico and Arizona and California. Not very many of them ever came — mostly soldiers to conquer the hapless Indians, and priests to convert them to Christianity. Even after two or three hundred years there were only a few thousand Spaniards in North America. Yet the Spanish influence lasted on, and Spanish is still the language of Mexico, and of a large part of Central and South America as well.

The French were the next to come. They were attracted by the rich fishing in the icy waters off Newfoundland and Nova Scotia, and by the beaver and other fur-bearing animals in the cold North. The French spread up the mighty river which they named the St. Lawrence, and to the Great Lakes. Then they paddled their long Indian canoes down strange rivers until they came to the Mississippi, the very Father of Waters. Down it they floated, all the way to its mouth, where they built the city of New Orleans, named after Orléans in Old France. Thus the French spread over a vast empire, but, like the Spaniards, they spread too thin. After almost two hundred years there were only sixty or seventy thousand Frenchmen in all the new country.

The English were the last to come, but they came to stay. They did not send over warriors, or missionaries either, but men and women who planned to make their homes in the New World. They had the great good luck to settle along the Atlantic coast between Maine and Florida. Here the climate was just right, and the soil was wonderfully rich. There were good harbors for ships, and swift rivers to turn the wheels of mills. The Indians of this region along the Atlantic coast were both few and weak. And within one or two hundred miles of the coast the great Appalachian mountain range reared up, serving as a barrier to fence the English in. This was the best thing that could have happened, for the English did not spread thin, as the Spaniards and French did, but stayed put and grew into strong communities.

At first there was only a trickle of settlers — tiny islands of people in a great ocean of forest. One feeble little colony in Virginia almost flickered out again and again. And again and again it was saved at the last moment, until in the end it grew to be the biggest and strongest of all the colonies. This first settlement was called Jamestown, named after King James I of England, just as Virginia itself was named after Elizabeth, the Virgin Queen. Another tiny colony, a little village named after Plymouth in England, was established by the Pilgrims on the cold sandy shores north of Cape Cod. Nine years later, in 1629, came a third settlement, again north of Cape Cod. This was the Puritan colony of Massachusetts Bay. Beginning in the 1620's, thousands of Puritans left England and settled the little towns of Salem and Boston and Cambridge, towns that are still flourishing.

Why did the settlers come? Why did they venture away from their homes in England, their families and their friends, to take the long trip across the perilous ocean to an unknown world? After all, it was a fearful risk to take. Why then did they keep coming?

For some it was adventure, the thing that still lures people to the far corners of the world, to explore the Arctic or climb the Himalayas or fly into outer space.

For some it was the promise of limitless riches. The Spaniards, after all, had found great stores of gold and silver. Who knew what might await fortune-hunters in America?

Others went out for the glory of their king or queen, to carry the flag of England with them, and plant a New England in America.

Most of them came, however, because they wanted to get away from their Old World and make a fresh start. In England or Scotland or Germany a man remained what he was born to be. If he was a farmer or a laborer, he remained a farmer or a laborer all his life, and the chances were that his children and their children would be farmers and laborers too. Most people were miserably poor, and knew that they would stay poor always. So the bolder of them took a chance on a better life in a New World. From the very beginning America was the land of the second chance.

There was one other reason why many settlers came to America — a reason that was especially strong with the Pilgrims and the Puritans who came to New England. That was religion. In each country of the Old World there was one church, and one church only, and everybody had to belong to that church. The Pilgrims who founded Plymouth, and the Puritans who came after them and founded Boston, were not happy with the Church of England. They wanted to worship God in their own way. So they sailed away to the New World where they could have their own churches and their own ministers, and find their own way to Heaven.

2.

How did they live in this New World, surrounded as they were by so many perils?

Many of them did not live. They died from strange new diseases or from starvation, from accidents or snakebites or Indian arrows — from all the things that can happen in a new country.

Many, too, got discouraged and went back to England. But there were always some who refused to give up. They learned to protect themselves from the Indians, or even to make friends with them. They learned how to dress warmly enough for the bitter winters and lightly enough for the hot summers, how to avoid snakebites and swamp fevers and other dangers from nature. They learned how to build wooden houses and get the right food, and soon they were living better than they had ever lived before. There were cod and mackerel in the sea, and the rivers swarmed with all kinds of fresh-water fish. There were deer everywhere, and bear; there were turkeys and partridges in the long grass; and wild geese and pigeons by the million, so thick they darkened the skies for hours. Fruit grew wild everywhere, and the trees were loaded down with nuts. Soon the settlers learned from the Indians to plant corn and pumpkins and squash, and they learned to raise tobacco, and to smoke it too.

Yes, the settlers could live well in America. And no matter how dangerous life was, it was free and exciting and there was a chance for everyone. So more and more people kept coming over, all of them eager to get away from the wars and poverty of the Old World.

Most of those who came over in the 1600's and the 1700's were English, but not all of them were. Wars and poverty sent over many Lowlanders and Highlanders from Scotland. Because they were bold and hardy they settled on the frontiers. Again and again it was a Scotsman who opened up the American wilderness.

Wars and poverty too sent thousands of poor Germans from the Rhine or the Black Forest to settle in New York and Pennsylvania. In the end there were so many of them that Pennsylvania seemed like another Germany, except that it was so free and so peaceful and so prosperous. German was spoken on the streets of the little towns that bore names like Bethlehem and Germantown. Out on the farms German farmers built great fat barns that looked as if they had come right out of the Black Forest, and on them they painted beautiful decorations.

There were Frenchmen, too, everywhere in the colonies. For when the French king announced in 1685 that he would not have any more Protestants in his country, thousands of French Protestants, who were called Huguenots, fled to Holland and England and finally found their way to America.

Then there were Dutch in New York, and Swedes in Delaware, and here and there some Danes and Swiss, and most important of all there were Negroes from Africa.

The Negroes had come over almost as soon as the whites, but not in the same way. It was just a few years after the first settlement in Virginia that a ship sailed up the James River with a cargo of Negro slaves from Africa. Because Virginia needed workers, and because the Negroes would work well in a hot climate, the colonists were glad to have them. As settlements moved down into the Carolinas and Georgia, one ship after another sailed in with its cargo of wretched slaves, torn from their families in Africa. And in time slavery spread all over the American colonies, to New England and New York and Pennsylvania as well as the South.

The new America that was coming into being in the 1700's was a big country, almost as big as the whole of Europe. As yet there weren't many people in this vast country — maybe one million after the first hundred years. But the population was growing faster than anywhere else in the world, for everybody seemed to have a family of eight or ten or twelve children.

Most of the Americans lived along the seacoast, farming the rich lands of the river valleys, or working in little towns like Boston or

New York or Philadelphia. Because the colonists lived so far away from the Mother Country they were forced to do almost everything for themselves. If an American wanted a house, he had to build it. If a group of farmers wanted a road, they had to cut down the trees and lay planks for the road. If they wanted schools for their children, they had to build a schoolhouse and find a teacher. If they wanted to worship, they had to form a congregation and build a church and get a preacher. They had to provide even the simplest things for themselves: leather for shoes, and wool for clothing. They had to defend themselves against Indians; they had to govern themselves. Life in the colonies was a constant training for being free and independent.

Life in the colonies had another very good effect: it tended to make most Americans pretty much alike. They had not been alike to start with. After all, they came from a great many countries of Europe, and from different classes of society; they spoke different languages, and had different religions. And in America they lived far apart from one another, for the distance from Massachusetts to South Carolina was as great as that from England to Italy or Spain. Yet this New World did not develop a lot of little Englands and Italys and Spains. Instead it developed one single country with one single people.

There were many reasons why Americans thought and acted alike. For one thing, they came to speak the same language: English. And they were all part of the British Empire, with the same king and queen.

Moreover, they had fought together in their own defense. All through the years the colonists had fought against the French in Canada and the Ohio country, and against the Indians on many a frontier; and there is nothing like fighting side by side to teach people to know and respect one another.

But perhaps most important, Americans acted and thought alike because they all lived much alike and had to meet and solve the same problems. Most of them were farmers or fishermen or lumberers; most of them were about as rich or as poor as their neighbors. They all had to make do in a new country, fit into that country, and live with it.

Some of the colonies had the good luck to have brave and energetic leaders. In Virginia it was John Smith who saved the day, at the very beginning. He was a soldier of fortune whose whole life was an extraordinary series of adventures. He had fought against the Turks and rescued princesses and escaped from jails and sailed the seven seas. Wherever there was adventure, wherever there was excitement, there you could be sure to find John Smith with his magnificent beard blowing in the wind. He sailed over to Virginia with the first group of settlers; he took charge of the new settlement. He made even the gentlemen work; and he fought the Indians and made treaties with them. And finally, according to him at least, he was saved most romantically by the Indian princess Pocahontas when he was taken prisoner by the Indians. Whether or not this ever happened, it is probably the most talked-of rescue in history!

The Pilgrim colony, up in Plymouth, had a very different kind of leader — not a soldier of fortune at all, but a pious and learned man, William Bradford. But some things Bradford had in common with Smith: a stout heart, a shrewd judgment, and a lively pen. As we have the Pocahontas story from Smith, so we have from Bradford stories like that of the First Thanksgiving in 1621, when a great feast was held and friendly Indians were invited.

Pennsylvania came later, and it too had the good fortune to have a generous and courageous leader, William Penn, who gave his name to the colony. He was a Quaker, and wanted to plant a colony in America where Quakers, and all others for that matter, could worship God as they pleased. He welcomed not only men and women of all religious faiths, but of all countries as well: Scotland, Wales, Germany, Switzerland, and others. Soon Pennsylvania was a melting pot of European people, and was changing them all into Americans.

Pennsylvania was the home of the greatest man from the colonial period: Benjamin Franklin. He had been born in Boston, to be sure, but he had made his way to Philadelphia as a boy of sixteen, and it was with that city that he cast his lot for the rest of his long life. A printer by trade, without any schooling to speak of, he became the most learned man and the most useful citizen in the colony, and finally in the whole of America. On his first day in little Philadelphia he walked down the cobbled streets munching on a big bun he had bought for his dinner, and wondering where he would get lodgings

and work. His industry, his shrewdness, his generosity brought him success, and when he was about forty years old he retired to devote the rest of his life to helping the people of his colony. Soon he had a hand in everything good and useful. He started the first library. He opened the first academy — it later became a great university. He organized a fire company, and he saw to it that the streets of the city were lighted and cleaned. He set up the first post office and served as postmaster for all the American colonies. He invented the Franklin stove, and musical glasses, and many other things. He experimented with electricity, flying a kite in a storm to prove that lightning and electricity were the same thing. He printed half a dozen newspapers. Each year he brought out an almanac — *Poor Richard's Almanac* he called it — that was read from Maine to Georgia. There it was that he wrote those sayings that even you know now: "Early to bed and early to rise, makes a man healthy, wealthy, and wise," for instance, or "One today is worth two tomorrows." For his son he wrote the story of his life, an *Autobiography* which was the first American book to be read all over the world, and which is still read with enjoyment today.

Later on, Franklin went to London to represent the American colonies. Though he lived in England a long time, he never lost his American simplicity or his American point of view. When he felt that the time had come for Americans to break away from their English parents and set up for themselves, he took the lead in working for independence.

It is time now that we turn to this story of how the American colonies became the independent United States.

3.

It was a spring day in the year 1775. A tall, red-headed Virginian was speaking to a little group of tense, eager men, gathered together from every one of the American colonies. "The distinctions between Virginians, New Yorkers, and New Englanders are no more," he said. "I am not a Virginian. I am an American." It was Patrick Henry, the orator whose words had stirred the Virginians again and again, and who was now speaking to the whole of America.

"Why stand we here idle?" he asked. "The war has actually begun. The next gale that sweeps from the north will bring to our ears the clash of resounding arms!" The next gale did just that. It brought news of the battles of Lexington and Concord, the opening battles of the War for American Independence.

What was it all about? How did it happen that the thirteen colonies were now, in 1775, fighting to become independent?

There always comes a time (nobody knows quite when or how) when children feel that they are grown up, and want to be independent. Mothers and fathers are rarely able to recognize this time when it comes. But this growing up and becoming independent is a law of life.

It is a law of history too. Colonies, like children, grow up and want to be independent. Mother countries hardly ever understand this. Usually they fight hard to keep their colonies as children.

A hundred and fifty years after England planted tiny settlements at Jamestown and Plymouth, the American colonies had grown up and wanted to be independent. Nobody seemed to know quite when or why this had happened, but that it had happened was clear enough. At least it was clear enough to Americans. It was not quite so clear to the English.

One reason that Americans felt ready for independence was a very simple one. It was that America was so much larger than England. As that firebrand Tom Paine wrote, "It is ridiculous for a continent to belong to an island." When you looked at the map and saw the little island that was England, and then looked on the other side of the Atlantic Ocean and saw the great sprawling continent that was America, it did indeed seem a bit ridiculous for a continent to belong to an island.

Of course there were more people on the island than on the continent — the English part of it, that is. Perhaps there were three or four times as many. But the American colonies were closing that gap very rapidly. By 1775 there were almost three million Americans, and their number was doubling every twenty-five years.

Size, then, was one reason why the Americans wanted to be on their own. Another reason was distance. It was three thousand miles from London to Boston, and a good many more to Charleston in South Carolina. And three thousand miles in those days was like three hundred thousand miles today. For you must not think of distance in terms of miles, but in terms of time. It took eight or ten weeks to get from England to America and, if the weather was bad, much longer.

Even this is not the whole story. After all, the English couldn't do much about size and distance. But there were other things that they could do something about, if they wanted to. Unfortunately for them, they didn't want to.

The real trouble was that the English made the Americans feel as if they were somehow inferior to the English, and unable to manage on their own. The English interfered constantly with the way the Americans ran their own affairs — their politics, their trade and commerce, their farming and lumbering and hunting, even their religion.

When Thomas Jefferson — another Virginian, like Patrick Henry — wrote the Declaration of Independence, he drew up a long list of all the injuries that the English had inflicted on the Americans, and he blamed them all on the English king, George III. Poor George III! He was full of good will and good intentions, and full of energy and industry too. In fact, he was far more of a busybody than he was a tyrant. He tried to do a great many things that he should have left alone, and the trouble was that he was neither very wise nor very clever.

Actually neither George III nor his ministers knew very much about the American colonies or seemed to care very much. They thought of themselves as devoted parents and they expected their colonies to be dutiful children. But they didn't bother to find out what were the real interests of the Americans. And as for the Americans, they thought of themselves not as children but as grownups, and felt that their first duty was to themselves, not to some distant king over in England.

After the end of the French and Indian War in 1763, misunderstandings came thick and fast. One year the Americans and the English would quarrel about the trade on the high seas; another year about taxes; another year about paying the expenses of keeping British soldiers in America; still another year about ownership of the rich lands in the Kentucky and Ohio country to the west. One thing led to another, as one thing will, and soon there was real trouble. For example, when some schoolboys of Boston pelted British soldiers with snowballs, and a few rocks too, the soldiers fired at them and killed and wounded several of them. This luckless affair was blown up into the "Boston Massacre," and soon most Americans all the way from Maine to Georgia were convinced that the redcoats had fired on innocent Bostonians just for the fun of it!

Or there was the exciting adventure of the Boston Tea Party. Americans of that time were great tea drinkers, like the British today. The English government put a tax on tea, and in protest Americans banded together and refused to drink it any more. When a ship weighed down with a cargo of tea sailed into Boston Harbor, one of

the local leaders, Samuel Adams, rallied his followers to action. Dressed as Mohawk Indians, all in war paint and feathers, they rushed down to the wharf and onto the ship, and dumped almost a thousand big boxes of tea into the water. For days you could drink Boston Harbor for your tea.

In the end it came to war. In the spring of 1775 Americans began to band together to resist what they called British tyranny. They formed companies of men who called themselves "minutemen" because they would be ready for action the minute they were called. They collected guns and gunpowder in warehouses in some of their towns. The British heard about this, and late one night in April the redcoats marched out of Boston toward the little towns of Lexington and Concord to surprise the Americans and seize their gunpowder. Tramp, tramp, tramp, they marched across the bridge over the Charles River, and out along the dusty roads, their bayonets gleaming in the moonlight.

No sooner had they started than an American patriot, Paul Revere (he made the loveliest silverware in America), dashed off to spread the alarm. "The British are coming," he cried, as he clattered down cob-

bled streets and along country roads to the little towns. And soon the minutemen were tumbling out of their beds and hurrying to their meeting places in the village squares. When the column of redcoats reached the little town of Lexington, they found a straggling group of minutemen drawn up on the village green to meet them. "If they mean to have a war, let it begin here," cried the Yankee Captain Parker, and when the shots rang out and a score of Americans fell, the war was on.

It lasted seven long years. It had started as a little skirmish in a Massachusetts village; when it was over it had changed the whole history of the world. Out of it came many things, but above all came a new nation, the United States of America.

How did the Americans manage to win their independence and set up a new nation?

In the beginning they had neither an army nor a navy. For that matter, they didn't even have a government. But all these things they put together quickly enough. First they got thirty-three-year-old Thomas Jefferson to draw up a Declaration of Independence. This tall, gangling, red-headed, freckle-faced Virginian could do anything, and do it well. He was a farmer, a lawyer, a scientist, an inventor, a musician, an architect, a scholar, and a dozen other things too; eventually he was President of the United States. Above all he was a statesman and a patriot who devoted sixty years of his life to the service of his country.

And for good measure Jefferson was the best writer in America. So, as it turned out, what he did best of all was just this task which Congress had put upon him: to write a Declaration of Independence. It was so beautifully written that within a short time almost everybody in the world came to know it. You probably know it yourselves:

> We hold these truths to be self-evident, that all men are created equal, that they are endowed by their Creator with certain unalienable Rights, that among these are Life, Liberty, and the pursuit of Happiness. That to secure these rights, Governments are instituted among Men, deriving their just powers from the consent of the governed. . . .

It was one thing to declare independence, and something else again to win it. But again the Americans did the very best thing they could possibly have done. They asked George Washington to take command of their armies. And just as Jefferson was the perfect choice of writer of the Declaration of Independence, Washington was the perfect choice of commander-in-chief.

He was still a young man then, tall and handsome, brave and steadfast, thoughtful and prudent. As a mere boy he had gone out to survey the forests and rivers of the wilderness West, living on the frontier and coming to know nature and the Indians. A little later he had fought under the British general, Braddock, in the first battle of the war with the French and Indians. Young Washington, who knew the Indians, warned Braddock against ambush, but the proud British general paid no attention. The Indians did ambush the army. Poor Braddock was killed and so were most of his officers, but Washington rode through the hail of arrows and bullets untouched. He had, so the Indians said, a charmed life.

After this war Washington retired to his great plantation, Mount Vernon, on the banks of the beautiful Potomac River. Here he lived in one of the handsomest houses in America. He raised tobacco and wheat on thousands of acres, and busied himself with the affairs of

his plantation and his church and his colony. This was what he enjoyed most — the quiet life of a farmer and a country gentleman. But after 1775 he was never again to have a really quiet life. For as soon as it became clear that there was going to be a war, the Americans put Washington in command of their armies. And after that they never let him get away from one kind of public service or another.

Washington was one reason why the Americans won their independence. Another reason was France. Off and on for over a hundred years the French had been fighting the English. The last time they had fought the English, in the French and Indian War, they had been badly beaten and had lost Canada to England. Naturally enough they wanted revenge, and now they saw their chance. As soon as it became clear that the Americans really meant to fight, France came in on their side. They sent over a number of young officers to help in the fighting, among them a handsome, brave young aristocrat: the Marquis de Lafayette. And what was more important, they sent over a fleet of warships.

The fighting, which had started on the little village green of Lexington in 1775, dragged on year after year. It spread from New England to New York, from New York to Pennsylvania; it broke out in the South — in Georgia and South Carolina; it swept up to the Old Dominion of Virginia. Again and again it seemed as if the British had triumphed; again and again it seemed as if the feeble American army would fall apart. But, inspired by George Washington, the Americans fought on. When things looked darkest, in 1777, the patriots caught the British army of General Burgoyne in the wilderness of upstate New York and captured the whole of it from "Gentleman Johnny," as Burgoyne was called, right down to the very horses and the baggage! It was this famous victory that brought France into the war — France, the ancient enemy of Britain and thirsting, now, for revenge.

In the end it was this combination of America and France that brought victory. For when in 1781 Lord Cornwallis at the head of an army of redcoats swept up through the Carolinas toward Virginia, Washington hurried down to meet him. And the French fleet hastened to support Washington.

Between them, Washington and the French bottled up the English general, Cornwallis, at Yorktown, down on the Virginia coast. Poor Cornwallis! He thought he was going to conquer all Virginia, and instead he found Washington's army in front of him and the French fleet in back of him, both of them firing on him night and day. In the end he had to surrender. His soldiers marched out in all their finery, the story goes, with their band playing "The World Turned Upside Down." So it seemed to the redcoats, but to Americans the world was very much right side up.

When the war was over, the Americans set up their own nation and their own government. They wrote a constitution, which the United States still has; it is now the oldest written constitution in the world. They wrote a Bill of Rights which gives everybody protection against tyranny. And with one voice they called on Washington to be the first President of the new nation. He had been first in war; now he was to be first in peace.

4.

Here then, in 1789, was the new United States, all fitted out with a brand-new Constitution, with a government, with a President — and, best of all perhaps, with land enough for everybody. For the United States of 1789 grew and grew. She grew so fast that even the map-makers could not keep up with her. In the beginning there were just thirteen colonies along the Atlantic coast. Then, after the Revolution, there was all the country between the Atlantic coast and the Mississippi River.

Even before the Revolution, eager pioneers like Daniel Boone had found their way out to the meadows and forests along the Ohio and Kentucky and Tennessee Rivers, and had sent back word that this was the richest and most beautiful country in all the world. For everything about this new western land was beautiful, and everything was on a large scale. The trees grew right up into the skies. The rivers were as broad as lakes, and the lakes as big as oceans. The soil was so rich that overnight corn grew higher than your head; the potatoes and turnips popped out of the ground; the squash and pumpkins grew so big it took two horses to haul them to market. There were so many deer you had to shoo them away, and the fish were so thick in the streams that you could walk right across a river on their backs and hardly even wet your feet. At least, that is the way the westerners talked about their country. It was an exaggeration, but it wasn't a very big exaggeration.

After the Revolution hundreds of men and women, discontented with life in the older settlements, struggled across the towering Appalachian Mountains to find new land that suited them. At first the whole trip west was made afoot, or on a wagon drawn by horses or oxen. Day after day, week after week, the pioneer families plodded along the dusty roads, or pushed their way over forest trails that were as likely as not overgrown with brush or littered with the limbs of trees, until at last they came to the great Appalachian Mountain barrier. Then up the mountains they toiled, in and out of dark valleys, along the banks of foaming streams and black lakes, until at last they came to the place where all the rivers ran to the west, and all the paths ran downhill. At Pittsburgh or some smaller town the weary pioneers stopped and put together a raft of logs, and on this they floated down the Ohio River, between banks of meadows and forests, until they came to a place that struck their fancy. There they beached their raft, unloaded their household goods, and set up housekeeping. Or if the land along the river was already taken, they pushed on into the interior until they found what they wanted. They clustered together in little villages, and around each village they raised a stockade of tall logs for protection against the savage Indians.

Remember, the Indians were still there — in the "dark and bloody ground" of Kentucky and Tennessee, or on the plains and prairies of the West. But in time they were driven away or killed off, and the western country opened to peaceful settlement. Then the little trickle of settlers turned into a stream and the stream into a great flood, as men and women and children poured over the mountains by the thousands and spread all over the great valley of the Ohio and the Mississippi Rivers.

After a while so many people wanted to go West that the government built roads for them to travel. Then, early in the century, came a wonderful invention, one that changed the whole history of the country. That was the steamboat.

It was Robert Fulton who built the first successful steamboat. He was a New York boy who wanted above everything else to be an artist. When he was twenty years old he went over to Paris to study painting. While he was there he became interested in engineering and built an iron bridge. Then he invented a submarine which nobody had any use for. His money ran out, so he came back to the United States and turned his talents to making a steamboat. On a bright summer day in 1807 his boat, the *Clermont,* steamed up the Hudson River from New York City to Albany. All along the banks of the lordly Hudson, people stood and waved their hats and cheered as the *Clermont* pushed its nose upstream, blowing out great billows of smoke from its smokestack. That was an important event in the history of New York. But

it was even more important out West, for it opened up the whole Mississippi Valley to settlement. All a person needed to do now was get out to Pittsburgh or the Great Lakes, and take a steamboat to where he wanted to go. And when he raised corn or wheat or tobacco, he could pack it up and put it on a steamboat and ship it off to market — all the way to Europe if he wanted to.

But there was still that business of getting out to Pittsburgh, or Buffalo, on the Great Lakes. At least there was for a while. Soon that problem was solved too — by building artificial rivers out to the West.

These were, of course, canals. The first big canal to be built in America, the Erie Canal, went all the way from the Hudson River to Lake Erie — a matter of almost four hundred miles.

The Erie Canal was such a success that soon other states began frantically digging canals. Pennsylvania built one even longer than the Erie — and harder to build too, for it had to go right through the mountains. And everywhere out West people set to work to dig canals — canals to link up Lake Erie and the Ohio River, or Lake Michigan and the Mississippi River. By the time they were through, there were dozens of places where a person could travel by boat from the Atlantic coast right out to the Mississippi.

After the steamboat came the steam train — the railroad. The first railroad tracks were laid just fifty years after the Declaration of Independence. The first trains were tiny little things, not much more than toys; they teetered dangerously on their iron tracks; they were open on the sides, and the locomotives blew great clouds of coal smoke into the faces of the hapless passengers, who were quickly covered with soot. And every so often the trains went off the rails, or caught fire, or something of that kind. But they went unbelievably fast — fifteen or twenty miles an hour — and they could go right up and down mountains. So they were a tremendous success, and soon almost everybody was riding on the railroads. Year after year the railroads snaked their way out West, up and down mountains, across rivers and through valleys, linking up city to city and state to state. Soon they had pushed all the way out to the Mississippi River and across into the prairie country beyond.

What with highways and canals and railroads, Americans filled up one West after another in record time. First they filled in the West on the other side of the Appalachian Mountains; then they filled in the West next to the Mississippi River; then they pushed across the Mississippi and started filling in what is now Missouri and Arkansas and Iowa. For by this time Thomas Jefferson was President, and he bought another enormous piece of territory in 1803. It was called Louisiana, but it was actually everything between the Mississippi River and the Rocky Mountains except Texas. The purchase doubled the size of the United States at one stroke. In no time at all — in fact, while Jefferson was still there to see it — the original thirteen states grew to twenty-three.

There weren't nearly enough Americans to settle all that land in the West and to do all the other things that a fast-growing country needed done. But help was on the way. From every country in Europe the boats sailed out, loaded down with people who wanted to start a new life in this New World. On they came, from England and Scotland and, most of all, from the run-down farms of poor Ireland. On they came, from the fishing villages of Norway and the mountain valleys of Sweden and the little islands of Denmark. On they came, from every farm and village and city of Germany, and from prim little canal towns of Holland and from deep valleys of Switzerland. They crowded onto rickety old boats, carrying all their worldly possessions in bundles; they lived for weeks and weeks on dry bread and dried meat and stale water; they stumbled hopefully off the boats onto the shores of America, worn out and sick, but with the light of hope in their eyes. They herded onto the new railroads or onto canal boats, and out West — out to the land of freedom, out to the land of plenty, out to the land of the future.

Soon the pioneers were calling for still more land. Soon the politicians were saying that it was the "manifest destiny" of the United States to own everything way out to the Pacific Ocean. Before you knew it, the Americans had made a treaty with England that gave them all of Oregon. And they had fought a war with Mexico and got all of Texas and California. Now the mapmakers had to redraw their maps all over again, and write "United States" across the whole continent, from the Atlantic Ocean to the Pacific Ocean. One thing you could say for the Americans: they certainly kept the mapmakers busy.

Even before the whole of this enormous territory was definitely part of the United States, American pioneers had started for it. Three streams of settlers moved out across the prairies and plains and mountains of the Far West. One of these streams flowed into Texas, and quickly made that country an American state; that was why it was so easy to take from Mexico. A second stream flowed in just the other direction, northward across some of the meanest mountains in the world, and down the Columbia River to Oregon. A third stream followed this same Oregon Trail until it came to the famous South Pass — the main pass through the first range of the Rocky Mountains — and then branched off to the Great Salt Lake. This third stream was made up of Mormons, who trudged way out to this distant country to find a land where they could worship as they pleased, just as the Pilgrims had done two hundred years earlier.

It had been hard to cross the Appalachians to Ohio and Kentucky, but it was harder yet to cross the whole of western America to Utah or Oregon or California. There were no railroads that far west, as yet, and no rivers or canals that anyone could use for travel. There were just "trails," to be followed on foot or, if you were lucky, or sick, in a covered wagon, pulled by skinny oxen who more often than not died on the way.

Going to the Far West meant walking 1,500 miles, through tall grass that cut your feet; across dangerous rivers where you might sink down into quicksand and drown; up dusty plateaus where there were no trees for shade, and no water either; through towering mountains where you might get lost or fall into a chasm or get caught in an early blizzard or starve to death or be shot by Indians. No wonder the trails to the West were marked by the skeletons of horses and oxen that had fallen on the way, and by the little white crosses on the graves of those who had died before they reached the land of their hopes.

For all this hardship, though, the settlement of Texas and Oregon and the Mormon state of Utah was a peaceful and orderly business — a matter of families moving out and setting up little farming communities for all the world like the ones they had left back East. But in 1849 came a westward movement so different from these that it was like the eruption of a volcano. California was the volcano, and it erupted with gold.

It was a mechanic named James Marshall who first found gold in California. He was a New Jersey man who had drifted halfway around the world to California, and was working on a big ranch belonging to the Swiss Johann Sutter when he spied a bright gold nugget in the bed of the American River. Soon "Gold" clanged out like a fire bell in the night. "Gold," cried the farmers and ranchers of old California, as they descended on poor Johann Sutter's ranch. "Gold," screamed the headlines of the newspapers all over the country. "Gold" — the

word ran up and down the frontier like a prairie fire, and farmers and mechanics threw down their tools and took the road to California. The fire spread to the busy cities of the Atlantic coast, and sober businessmen gave up their jobs and took off for El Dorado. It leaped across the Atlantic and ran up and down the countries of the Old World, and fortune hunters poured into every seaport and crowded on every ship and ploughed across the Atlantic and around the Horn and up the long coast of South America to California. The whole world, it seemed, was singing

> O, Susannah, don't you cry for me,
> For I'm off to California with a washbowl on my knee!

Within two years a hundred thousand men and women — mostly men — had fought their way to the magic land to find gold. Not many of them did find it; but, as it turned out, California was much richer in other things than it was in gold. So the gold seekers stayed on, farming and ranching and working at a thousand different jobs, and building a new America along the Pacific coast.

Texas and Oregon, the plains and the mountains, the Iowa prairie and the blue grass of Kentucky, the wheat fields of the North and the cotton fields of the South — many different countries were packed together into one United States. And it wasn't just that the various parts of the country were different. The people were different too — different, that is, in character and interests. They were from many lands, and there were Protestants and Catholics and Jews. There were farmers and workingmen and businessmen, just as in other countries;

and there were frontiersmen and Indian fighters and gold miners and rivermen and cowboys, not at all as in other countries, but only in the United States.

There were rich merchants like the German immigrant John Jacob Astor, who owned most of the furs that were trapped all over the West. There were scholars like Noah Webster who put together a Blue-backed Speller that every schoolboy and schoolgirl in America studied — and then put together a Dictionary that we still use today. There were artists like John James Audubon, who had been born in Haiti and studied in France and came over to America to make paintings of birds so beautiful that you expected the birds to fly right off the paper and into the sky. There were pioneers like Davy Crockett, who could shoot a squirrel in the eye at one hundred yards, and tell the tallest tales anyone ever heard, and who died fighting at the Alamo for the independence of Texas. There were sailors like Richard Cleveland of Salem, who at the age of twenty-one sailed a series of tiny ships twice around the world, trading, exploring, and fighting, putting down a mutiny in the China seas, fighting pirates in the waters off Malaya, shooting it out with Mexicans in California — and retiring at the age of twenty-seven. There were kind-hearted idealists like Johnny Appleseed of Massachusetts, who wandered through the Ohio country, planting apple and cherry and pear trees wherever he went.

And there were great soldiers like Robert E. Lee of Virginia, and poor frontier lawyers like Abe Lincoln of Illinois, who played such a great part in the next chapter of American history — the saddest and in some ways the most splendid chapter of all: the Civil War.

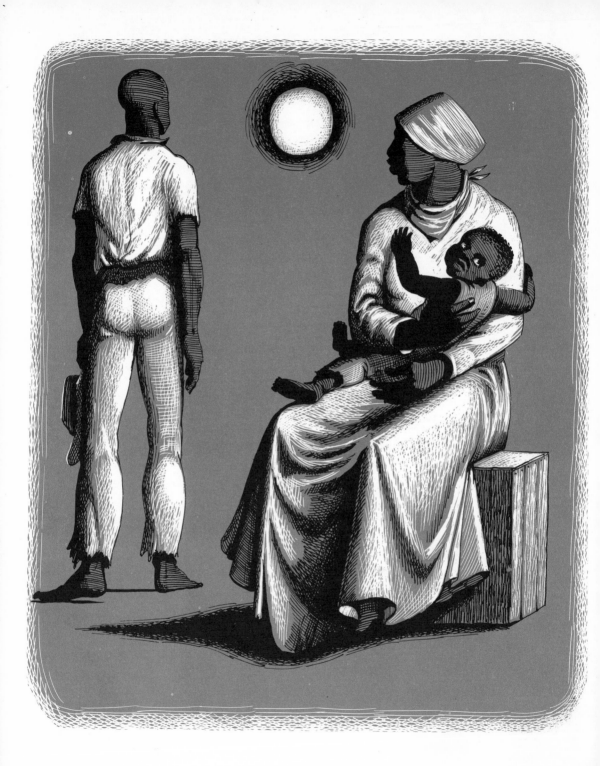

5.

The United States was an immense country, and it was no wonder that different sections and regions bickered and quarreled, just as different nations in Europe bickered and quarreled and even fought. But up to the time of the settlement of Oregon and California none of the quarrels had been serious enough to break up the American family. In fact, most of the quarrels — such as who was to have the land in the West, or where the railroads were to go, or how the government was to be run — had pretty much solved themselves. But now came a quarrel that did not solve itself, but went on and on, and grew hotter and hotter every year.

That quarrel was slavery.

Slavery was an old story in America. The first Spaniards who came over to the Caribbean islands made slaves of the Indians, and when the poor Indians were killed off, the Spaniards brought in Negroes from Africa to take their places. A few years after the English had settled in Jamestown the Dutch brought in a cargo of Negro slaves, and before long slavery had spread all over the colonies. But slavery didn't work well in the North, so it gradually died out there. In the South, however, where the climate was hot, and where slaves could work together raising tobacco or picking cotton, slavery caught on and grew. By 1860 there were almost four million slaves in the South: one out of every three people there was a slave.

Most of the men and women of the South took slavery for granted. It was what they were used to, and they didn't see anything wrong with it. But more and more men and women in the North thought it was wrong for one man to own another.

One of the people who thought slavery was wrong was a frail little lady named Harriet Beecher Stowe. Though she came originally from New England, she lived in Cincinnati, on the Ohio River right across from the slave state of Kentucky. Many of the slaves tried to swim or paddle across the Ohio River to the North and freedom, and of course sometimes their masters found them and took them back to slavery.

Mrs. Stowe couldn't help seeing some of all this in the streets of Cincinnati, and she became so disturbed by the whole question of slavery that she wrote a story about it, which she called *Uncle Tom's Cabin*. It portrayed the saintly Negro Uncle Tom and the slave girl Eliza and the beautiful little Eva and her slave companion Topsy. Soon people all over the world were reading *Uncle Tom's Cabin* and feeling sorry for both the slaves and their masters.

Stories like this made people everywhere want to put an end to slavery — people everywhere but in the South, that is. Most of the southerners were good to their slaves, and they couldn't understand why everybody outside the South wanted to interfere with what they felt was their business. Gradually they came to think that the only way they could keep their own way of life was to separate from the North and set up as an independent country.

HARRIET BEECHER STOWE

But to break up the American Union was a very serious thing. It was like breaking up not one but several million families, all at once. And to make it worse, this separation was a one-sided affair. Northerners didn't want to separate. They wanted to keep the old Union "one and indivisible." If the South tried to break away, the North was ready to fight to keep the Union together.

The South did try. In the spring of 1861 eleven Southern States pulled out of the Union and set up as the Confederate States of America. They wrote themselves a new constitution; they elected Jefferson Davis of Mississippi as their President; they even got themselves a new flag: the beautiful Stars and Bars.

Now the die was cast. Would it be peace or war? Would it be one nation or two? Would it be freedom for the Negro or slavery?

Abraham Lincoln was President when all this happened. He was a son of the frontier — of early Kentucky. His family had crossed the river to Indiana, and from there he had drifted to Illinois, where he chopped logs and waited on store, and taught himself law, and hung out his shingle as a lawyer, and finally went into politics. Awkward in appearance, he was gentle, honest, brave, and humble, and he had the ability to get along with almost everybody. He had a talent for telling stories, and a great sense of fun. He could argue cases, and win them. He could make speeches that lifted people right out of themselves. And he had a passion for what was fair and what was just and what was right.

When Lincoln took office as President in 1861, he became the leader of the North. He was a man of peace, but he would not give up the

ABRAHAM LINCOLN

Union without a fight. When, on a beautiful April morning in 1861, southern soldiers opened fire on the Stars and Stripes waving over Fort Sumter in the harbor of Charleston, South Carolina, Lincoln called for volunteers to fight for the Union. The war was on.

What a war it was! For four terrible years northern boys in blue fought southern boys in gray, until the very rivers seemed to run with blood and the thunder of cannon drowned out the thunder from the skies. Most of the soldiers really *were* boys, of sixteen or seventeen or eighteen, boys from farms and factories who had never before worn a uniform or carried a gun. Lincoln raised one great army after another; the armies marched south, across the Potomac or the Ohio into Virginia and Kentucky and on into any part of the South they could reach.

The Confederacy raised army after army, and put their armies under the command of Robert E. Lee. He turned out to be one of the greatest generals in history. Lee was a Virginian, born in a great stone plantation house called Stratford, on the banks of the Rappahannock. His father had been one of Washington's generals: the famous "Light-Horse Harry" Lee; and from the beginning Robert took it for granted that he too would be a soldier. He went to the Military Academy at West Point, and for four years stood first in his class, and was graduated without a single mark against him!

Robert E. Lee was as handsome and distinguished and polished as Abraham Lincoln was awkward and gangling and homely. He had many slaves, but freed them all because he did not like slavery. He was a splendid soldier, but he did not like soldiering — or war, either. But he was brave and gallant, and he loved the South. When trouble came, he became the southern leader.

Different as Lee and Lincoln were, they were both fine men of great character. America was fortunate to have such leaders in this terrible time.

Never had there been such courage, or such devotion to a cause. The Yankees poured into the South, long lines of blue fording the rivers and surging along dusty roads, singing "John Brown's body lies a-mold'ring in the grave," or, more often, "We'll hang Jeff Davis on a sour apple tree."

And the Rebs, as they were called, the boys in gray, gathered from all over the South to meet the invaders. The southerners stood guard at bridges; put out pickets to tell when the enemy was near; dug trenches to protect themselves from bullets. They had their own songs too — wonderful songs like "Dixie," or "Maryland, My Maryland," or "The Bonnie Blue Flag."

Hurrah! Hurrah! for southern rights, hurrah,
Hurrah for the bonnie blue flag that bears a single star.

The armies hurled themselves at each other in one tremendous battle after another: Bull Run, and Antietam, and Shiloh, and Gettysburg — just names to us now, but names that spelled bravery and

ROBERT E. LEE

gallantry and glory and death to thousands and thousands of boys in blue and in gray.

The war dragged on, with fighting in the wilderness of Virginia, in the mountains of Tennessee, along the muddy waters of the Mississippi, in the bright clear waters of the Gulf of Mexico, and on the high seas. The losses grew bigger and bigger, and there was sorrow in thousands of homes. General Lee fought with superb skill, and his soldiers with dauntless courage, but the Union found able generals too — men like William Tecumseh Sherman and Ulysses S. Grant — and the Billy Yanks were just as courageous as the Johnny Rebs. The North was much larger than the South and could put many more soldiers into the field. So, in the end, numbers counted. When Union armies had crisscrossed the whole of the South; when Union navies had bottled up all the southern ports; and when General Grant had surrounded the army of General Lee, the South had to admit defeat.

If it had not been for Lee, the South could not have held out so long

or so gallantly. If it had not been for Lincoln, the North might never have fought on through defeats and setbacks to final victory. But perhaps the greatest thing about both of these men is that they never gave way to hatred. Lincoln would not even use the word "enemy" to describe the Confederates, because he wanted to live with them again as members of one family. In his last speech he asked everyone to show "malice toward none, charity for all." And Lee, too, avoided hatred and bitterness and set an example of chivalry that has never been surpassed.

Millions of southerners mourned the "lost cause," but everyone now admits that it was a good thing that the war ended as it did. The victory of the North meant two things of importance. It meant the end of slavery in America. During the war Lincoln had freed the slaves. That is why he is sometimes known as the "Great Emancipator." And it meant that the United States would be one great and united nation, ready to play her part in the world of free nations.

6.

After the Civil War the United States settled down once again to the serious business of growing. Never had a people been more busy! They rebuilt the cities that had been destroyed by armies; they flung railroads clear across the continent to Texas and California and Puget Sound way up on the Pacific coast. They felled trees and built factories; they dug in the earth for gold and silver and, what was far more valuable, for iron ore and coal. Everything grew fast — farms and factories, old cities like New York and Boston, and new cities like Chicago and Detroit.

Everybody helped in this building up of America — farmers who grew wheat and corn for the whole world; workingmen who made threshing machines and railroad cars; businessmen and bankers who raised the money and managed the industries; schoolteachers who taught the millions of children; and, for that matter, artists and writers who made life pleasant for all the others. No group, however, contributed more than the inventors, who every day came up with some new machine or some new method of doing things twice as fast and twice as cheaply and easily as before.

Americans seemed particularly clever about inventing new ways of doing old things. One of them found out how to make steel out of iron. Another put together a threshing machine that would thresh as much wheat in an hour as four men could in a whole day. Another found out how to make rubber hard, so that it could be used for a thousand things. Still another invented the telephone.

The most inventive of all Americans was a man named Thomas Edison. When he was still a boy, he began tinkering with machinery and seeing what he could do with electricity. He was too poor to go to school, so he sold newspapers and candy on trains. Soon he was busy inventing — a new idea every day. He invented the phonograph, the electric incandescent lamp, a motion picture machine, and hundreds of other things hardly less useful, so that in the end he became both rich and famous.

All these new farms and railroads and factories and inventions meant, in the end, better living for almost everybody. There were more goods and more work, and for the first time in history there was beginning to be enough to go round. More people than ever before could be sure of having enough to eat and a warm room to sleep in and shoes and stockings to wear in the wintertime.

But industry and invention meant something more than just food and clothing and comforts, important as they are. Industry and invention meant that people could satisfy their needs more easily, so that they no longer had to work long, long hours from dawn to dark, but had time for school and play and rest. For most people life was becoming pleasanter and easier than it had ever been before.

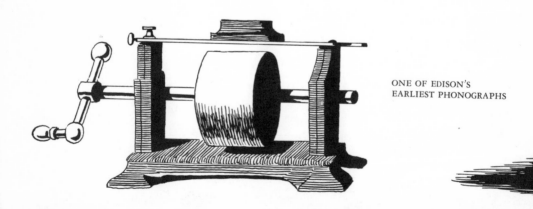

ONE OF EDISON'S
EARLIEST PHONOGRAPHS

A country growing as fast as the United States needed still more and more people to do all the work that was to be done, and fortunately most of Europe seemed ready to come over and help. Italians, Rumanians, Hungarians, Poles, Irish people, Swedish people, and those from dozens of other countries — on they came by the thousands, by

THOMAS EDISON

the hundred thousands, by the millions, and America took them in like a big sponge takes up water.

One of these newcomers landed at Castle Island in New York with his mother and father in 1848, even before the Civil War. He was nothing but a boy, a little fellow of twelve, with pink cheeks, blue eyes, hair that was almost white, and a brogue so broad you could almost cut it with a knife. His name was Andrew Carnegie, and he had come over from Scotland. Like many of the immigrants he brought with him nothing but energy, a quick wit, and a good mind and character.

The Carnegie family went out to Pittsburgh, and soon Andy was working in a telegraph office. Before he was twenty-five he was put in charge of all the telegraphs of the eastern part of the United States, and during the Civil War he took care of the important telegrams to the armies and to President Lincoln. A few years later Carnegie was making iron and steel, and in another ten years he was the owner of the greatest steel works in the whole world, so rich he could hardly keep track of his money.

Just making money isn't very interesting, but that isn't the whole of Andrew Carnegie's story. He loved learning. He had been far too poor to go to school, and he had educated himself. Now he determined to use his money to help others educate themselves. He gave hundreds of millions of dollars to build Carnegie libraries in towns and cities throughout the country. On top of that he gave millions to universities, not forgetting those back in Scotland. Carnegie admired bravery, and he provided gold medals to be given for special acts of heroism.

But more than anything else Andrew Carnegie was interested in peace. He had been in the middle of the American Civil War, and he knew that machinery and science and new inventions would make new wars far worse, even, than that one. So he put aside part of his great fortune to set up a court which should settle quarrels between nations by law, just as courts settle quarrels between neighbors.

For alas, the bigger and stronger most nations became, the more they seemed to quarrel and fight. The United States had been lucky in staying out of most of the great wars of the eighteenth century, but even the United States had fought with Great Britain in 1812, and with Mexico in 1848, and had fought a great civil war in 1861. After that there was a long stretch of peace, except for a short war with Spain in 1898.

The United States went into that war to help free the island of Cuba from Spain, which was oppressing the Cubans. The whole war was over in three or four months, and at its end the United States found herself with the islands of Cuba and Puerto Rico on her hands, and, way off in the Pacific, the Philippine Islands.

The United States didn't want these islands as colonies, for Americans remembered when they had been colonials. So the United States gave Cuba back to the Cubans. Then, after a long wait, she set up the Philippine Islands as an independent country. Puerto Rico was different; she, and the Hawaiian Islands in the Pacific also, wanted to be part of the United States. And, sure enough, Puerto Rico was brought in as a United States possession, and in 1959 Hawaii became the fiftieth state of the Union.

Hawaii had hoped to be the forty-ninth state, but Alaska beat her to it by just a few months. Secretary of State Seward bought Alaska from the Russians way back in 1868; it was known then as "Seward's Folly." But after a while gold was discovered in Alaska, and thousands of prospectors flooded up to the Klondike gold fields, just as they had flooded out to California back in the forties and fifties. And, again just as with California, once the settlers were there, they discovered farming and fishing and all sorts of things. And in time there were enough people up in Alaska to make a state, and they hammered on the doors of statehood just as loudly as did the Hawaiians.

Now the United States began to take her place as a power in the world, alongside ancient nations such as England and France and Russia, and newer nations such as Italy and Germany. In 1914 Germany, a great military power bent on conquering other nations, plunged into war against Great Britain and France. The United States tried to stay aloof, but it soon became clear that Great Britain and France needed help. So, after the fighting had raged for three years, the President of the United States, Woodrow Wilson, led his country into the war. Soon American food was flowing into England; soon American soldiers in khaki were flooding into France, where they helped turn the tide of battle. Germany was defeated.

The end of this war, World War I, found the United States the one great nation that had not been damaged by fighting and had not lost millions of her sons. She came out of the war the strongest and most prosperous of all countries. From being merely one of many world powers, the United States became the first world power.

Yet for a time the United States was unwilling to play a part in world affairs. She had for so long been in the habit of minding only her own affairs that she found it hard to be concerned with what went on in other countries.

And in truth there seemed enough to do at home. Ten years after the end of the war hard times came all over the world — and in the United States too. Millions of men were out of work; factories closed down; stores shut up; there were long bread lines and soup kitchens for those who did not even have enough to eat. All of a sudden it seemed that the rich American nation was not rich at all.

FRANKLIN DELANO ROOSEVELT

For a time, things were at a standstill. Then a great leader appeared: Franklin Delano Roosevelt. His life was like a fairy tale. He had been born to wealth in a beautiful big house on the banks of the Hudson River. He had the best education that America and Europe could give. He went into politics and rose rapidly until he was running the United States Navy in World War I. He seemed headed for the White House, like his distant cousin Theodore Roosevelt, who had twice been President. Then, when everything looked best, Franklin Roosevelt was stricken with polio. But he did not give way to despair. Year after year he fought his way back to health, though he never did get to the point where he could walk without crutches. He was chosen Governor of New York, and because he did so well as Governor, he was elected President in 1932, when times were darkest. He stayed President longer than any other man in the history of the United States — twelve years!

There were two things that President Roosevelt had to do. First, he had to cure the hard times and get men and women back to work. Second, he had to get the machinery of government and business and labor and farming all working smoothly again. Both of these things he managed to do in his first two terms as President. Then he faced a third problem, one even more serious than the other two. That was the problem of helping save England and Europe from conquest and ruin.

For once again the Old World had plunged into war — a war

fought by more countries and more people than even World War I. Germany had fallen under the control of Adolf Hitler, the worst tyrant in history. Hitler wanted to conquer all the other countries of Europe; he wanted to rule the whole world. By 1941, with the help of Japan, he was well on the way to doing these things. Once again, as back in 1916, Great Britain and France were in mortal danger. And once again it was the United States that stepped in to help them. For President Roosevelt saw that if the tyrant Hitler won, the whole world might go back to the Dark Ages.

This was the biggest and fiercest war in history. American soldiers and sailors and airmen fought all over the globe. The United States, in fact, fought three wars. One was against Japan, and it was fought all over the broad Pacific Ocean, and in the islands of the Far East, and in strange countries like Burma and Malaya, and on Japan itself. A second was against Italy; that was fought in North Africa and on the ancient island of Sicily and up seven hundred miles of Italy, through mountains that towered to the skies. A third war — the one

that finally counted most — was fought against Germany. This was fought first in the lands that German armies had conquered: France and Belgium and the Netherlands. Then it was fought on the soil of Germany and in the skies over every German city.

In the end America and her brave allies won all of these wars. Freedom lived once again in Europe, and had a new birth on other continents.

If World War I had made the United States a great world power, World War II made her even greater. By 1956 the United States stood forth as the most powerful nation in all history.

Yes, America had come a long way since John Smith planted a tiny colony in Jamestown and William Bradford and his Pilgrims fell on their knees and prayed on the shores of Cape Cod. She had come a long way since Thomas Jefferson wrote the Declaration of Independence and Cornwallis surrendered at Yorktown; since pioneers toiled on foot out to Texas and Oregon and California; since Lincoln freed the slaves and saved the Union.

America had come a long way — but there was still a long way to go. For freedom is never completely won, but must be won anew by each generation. And freedom means not only freedom from tyranny or slavery, but freedom to grow up in a world of peace. So there is still plenty to do.

All that you have read is merely preparation for the future.

There is no reason why that future should not be even more wonderful than the past.

But that is up to you.

INDEX

IN CONGRE

nous Declaration of the

When in the Course of human events, it becomes necessary

...e separate and equal station to which the Laws of Nature and

...them to the separation . ——————— We hold these

...among these are Life, Liberty and the pursuit of Happiness

... — That whenever any Form of Government becomes destructi...

...uch principles and organizing its powers in such form, a...

...lished should not be changed for light and transient causes;

...elves by abolishing the forms to which they are accustomed .

...absolute Despotism, it is their right, it is their duty, to throw...

...nies; and such is now the necessity which constrains them to...

...and usurpations, all having in direct object the establishment...

...used his Assent to Laws, the most wholesome and necessary

SS, JULY 4, 1776.

States of Am

en united

people to dissolve the political bands which have connected them

re's God entitle them, a decent respect to the opinions of man

to is self-evident, that all men are created equal, that they are

that to secure these rights, Governments are instituted among

these ends, it is the Right of the People to alter or to abolish it,

m shall seem most likely to effect their Safety and Happine

cordingly all experience hath shewn, that mankind are m

when a long train of abuses and usurpations, pursuing inva

h Government, and to provide new Guards for their future s

heir former Systems of Government. The history of the p

absolute Tyranny over these States. To prove this, let Fa

ublic good. ——————— He has forbidden his Governors to